INVESTIGATING SCIENCE

Five Senses

Preschool–Kindergarten

Table of Contents

www.themailbox.com

©2003 by THE EDUCATION CENTER, INC.
All rights reserved.
ISBN# 1-56234-542-7

Manufactured in the United States
10 9 8 7 6 5 4 3 2 1

Five Senses

Managing Editor: Cindy K. Daoust
Editor at Large: Diane Badden
Staff Editor: Kelly Coder
Contributing Writers: Beth Allison, Lori Alisa Burrow, Susan DeRiso, Heather Lynn Miller
Copy Editors: Tazmen Carlisle, Gina Farago, Karen Brewer Grossman, Amy Kirtley-Hill, Karen L. Mayworth, Kristy Parton, Debbie Shoffner
Cover Artist: Clevell Harris
Art Coordinator: Greg D. Rieves
Artists: Pam Crane, Theresa Lewis Goode, Nick Greenwood, Clevell Harris, Ivy L. Koonce, Sheila Krill, Clint Moore, Greg D. Rieves, Rebecca Saunders, Barry Slate, Donna K. Teal

The Mailbox® Books.com: Jennifer Tipton Bennett (DESIGNER/ARTIST); Stuart Smith (PRODUCTION ARTIST); Karen White (EDITORIAL ASSISTANT); Paul Fleetwood, Xiaoyun Wu (SYSTEMS)

President, The Mailbox Book Company™: Joseph C. Bucci
Director of Book Planning and Development: Chris Poindexter
Curriculum Director: Karen P. Shelton
Book Development Managers: Cayce Guiliano, Elizabeth H. Lindsay, Thad McLaurin

Editorial Planning: Kimberley Bruck (MANAGER); Debra Liverman, Sharon Murphy, Susan Walker (TEAM LEADERS)
Editorial and Freelance Management: Karen A. Brudnak; Hope Rodgers (editorial assistant)
Editorial Production: Lisa K. Pitts (TRAFFIC MANAGER); Lynette Dickerson (TYPE SYSTEMS); Mark Rainey (TYPESETTER)
Librarian: Dorothy C. McKinney

More great science books from *The Mailbox®*:

About This Book

Welcome to *Investigating Science—Five Senses*! This book is one of six must-have resource books that support the National Science Education Standards and are designed to supplement and enhance your existing science curriculum. Packed with practical cross-curricular ideas and thought-provoking reproducibles, these all-new, content-specific resource books provide preschool and kindergarten teachers with a collection of innovative and fun activities for teaching thematic science units.

Included in this book:
Investigating Science—Five Senses contains five cross-curricular thematic units, each containing
- Background information for the teacher
- Easy-to-implement instructions for science experiments and projects
- Student-centered activities and reproducibles
- Literature links
- Easy-to-use icons

 Sense of smell   Sense of hearing

 Sense of sight   Sense of touch

 Sense of taste   Multiple senses

Cross-curricular thematic units found in this book:
- Five Senses at the Zoo
- Five Senses at the Bakery
- Five Senses in the Garden
- Five Senses in the Woods
- Five Senses at Home

Five Senses at the Zoo

Youngsters will go wild over the animal-related activities in this "sen-zoo-ry" unit!

Background for the Teacher

- The five main external senses (sight, hearing, smell, taste, touch) help us understand what is happening in our environment. Each sense is controlled by a different sense organ (eyes, ears, nose, tongue, skin).
- Sight is the most important sense for learning about the world around us. We use our eyes in almost everything we do.
- Hearing makes it possible for us to communicate with others through speech. Hearing also alerts us to danger and provides pleasure such as listening to music.
- Smelling helps us recognize what is happening around us and helps us recognize food. Smell is closely related to taste because we usually smell and taste food at the same time.
- Tasting food helps determine what and how much we eat. We often smell and taste food simultaneously, so when we have a stuffy nose some foods may taste similar.
- Touching helps us determine the shape and texture of objects. We can also feel warmth, coldness, and pain through touch.

Put Me in the Zoo!
(Comparing Similarities and Differences)

Youngsters will stand in line to join this wild activity as they compare the five sensory organs of an animal to those of a person. In advance, gather a variety of magazines with pictures of animals and people, a large sheet of bulletin board paper, scissors, and glue. Draw a simple zoo cage on the bulletin board paper as shown. Discuss with youngsters the five senses and the body part used for each sense *(eyes, ears, nose, hands, tongue)*. Then have each child cut out several magazine pictures of animal and human body parts associated with the five senses. As a class, observe the pictures of animal ears and human ears; then discuss how they are similar and how they are different. You may want to record students' answers on a chart. Repeat the comparison activity with each remaining body part. Then invite small groups of youngsters to glue their body part cutouts onto the zoo cage to create silly mixed-up characters. Title the bulletin board paper "Our Mixed-Up Zoo" and display for all to enjoy.

Zoo Tales

Animal Senses: How Animals See, Hear, Taste, Smell and Feel by Pamela Hickman
Busy Bunnies' Five Senses by Teddy Slater
A Children's Zoo by Tana Hoban
My Visit to the Zoo by Aliki
Touch by Sue Hurwitz

Our Mixed-Up Zoo

The Petting Zoo
(Fine-Motor Skills, Sense of Touch)

Do pet these animals! This fun flap booklet will tickle youngsters' sense of touch as they compare animal coverings. Read the text on each booklet page to students and then help them follow the directions below. (For safety reasons, remind each child not to put any of the art materials into his mouth.)

Materials for each child:
copy of pages 9–12
small colorful feather
1" square of sandpaper
1" square of faux fur
1" square of a latex glove
scissors
glue
crayons

Look up in a tree to see my colorful feathers! 1

Look at me! I am king of the jungle with very soft fur. Don't you agree?

In the water I swim free. My skin is rough, just like me! 3

Directions:
1. Color and cut out booklet page 1 and the corresponding flap. Glue the feather onto the parrot. Glue the flap where indicated.
2. Color and cut out booklet page 2 and the corresponding flap. Glue the fur onto the square. Glue the flap where indicated.
3. Color and cut out booklet page 3 and the corresponding flap. Glue the sandpaper onto the square. Glue the flap where indicated.
4. Color and cut out booklet page 4 and the corresponding flap. Glue the latex onto the square. Glue the flap where indicated.
5. Draw yourself in the space provided on booklet page 5. Color and cut out the page.
6. Personalize, color, and cut out the booklet cover. Then sequence the pages and staple them together along the left side.
7. Share the booklet with a partner and compare how your skin feels to how each animal's skin feels.

Leaping out of the water is fun to me. My skin is smooth as can be! 4

The zoo has many animals to see. But not one animal feels like me! 5

The Do-Touch Zoo!

name Ashley

5

Follow Your Nose
(Language Activity, Sense of Smell)

Pretending to be a zoo animal sniffing to identify a snack will help youngsters understand the importance of the sense of smell. To prepare, collect enough egg cartons to cut out a class supply of single egg cups. Also gather ribbon and a selection of aromatic foods that zoo animals may eat, such as oranges, apples, bananas, spinach leaves, and tuna. Put each type of food into a separate resealable plastic bag. Next, give each child an egg cup and have him decorate it to resemble the nose of his favorite zoo animal. Help each child punch a hole in each side of the cup and then tie on two lengths of ribbon as shown. Then have him hold his animal nose in place as you tie the ribbon around his head.

Invite each of your little zoo friends to sit in a circle on the floor. Then ask them to close their eyes as you pass around a bag of food. Ask each child to sniff the food and then say a descriptive word about its smell. Record students' answers on a chart. After each child has had a turn, ask each to guess the identity of the food. Repeat with each remaining bag of food. Then discuss with youngsters how animals use their sense of smell to find food.

To the Point
(Sorting, Classifying)

Tickle, tickle, tickle! Whiskers and antennae may tickle us, but one of their real purposes is to help an animal detect movements and vibrations. To prepare, cut in half one paper plate for each child, and then staple one half onto each remaining paper plate to create two sorting pockets as shown. Discuss with youngsters some of the uses for whiskers and antennae (see examples below). Give each child her sorting pockets and the materials listed. Have her use the paper strips and crayons to decorate one pocket to resemble an animal with whiskers and decorate the other pocket to resemble an animal with antennae as shown. Ask each child to color and cut out her picture cards. Have her sort the picture cards into two groups: those with whiskers and those with antennae. Then have her place each picture in the corresponding pocket. Twitch, twitch!

> **Materials for each child:**
> copy of page 13
> 3 small paper plates
> several black construction paper strips
> scissors
> crayons
> access to a stapler

> Whiskers help a cat protect its eyes, move in darkness, and detect changes in wind direction.
> A walrus pokes its whiskers into the ocean bottom to feel for clams or crabs; then it digs them up with its tusks.
> Insects, lobsters, and crabs may use antennae to sense vibrations and heat.
> Some insects use antennae for the sense of smell.

I'm All Ears!
(Experiment, Sense of Hearing)

This "ear-y" activity will teach youngsters that large ears can be a positive attribute. Explain to students that the outer part of the ear, the *auricle,* helps in hearing because it gathers sound and sends it to the *eardrum.* Some animals (such as elephants, hares, bats, and foxes) have large ears that help increase their sense of hearing. Have each child hold one cup close to her ear and then experiment listening to different sounds (music, talking, outdoor noises, etc.). Ask her to compare the difference in listening to sounds using the cup and listening to sounds without the cup. Then have her follow the directions below to create a sound-absorbing animal ears headband.

Materials for each child:
two 9 oz. paper cups with the bottom cut out
construction paper (color depends on child's chosen animal)
construction paper headband, sized to fit child's head
scissors
crayons
access to tape

Directions:
1. On a colored sheet of construction paper, draw a pair of animal ears (elephant, fox, hare, bat, etc.) and cut them out.
2. Tape one ear onto each cup.
3. Tape each cup onto the headband as shown. (Make sure cups are located where your ears will be.)
4. Wear your animal ears to experiment listening to different sounds.

Lend Me Your Ears
(Listening Skills)

Youngsters will learn why a keen sense of hearing helps animals survive in the wild. In advance, gather a tray, chart paper, and different noise-making items (whistle, bell, rhythm sticks, rain stick or a plastic bottle filled with rice, cymbals or two pan lids, etc.). Place the objects on the tray. Invite youngsters to gather on the carpet and ask them to listen as you identify and make a sound with each item. Then place the tray of items in another room (or out of sight in another section of the classroom). Have one child at a time go to the items and choose one to make a sound as the rest of the class listens intently. Challenge youngsters to name the item making the sound. If desired, have youngsters compare the intensity of each sound by wearing their animal headbands from "I'm All Ears!" on this page. Then discuss with students how listening helps animals survive. *(Listening helps them hear other animals or people who may harm them, and it helps them hunt for food.)*

Monkey See, Monkey Do
(Matching Body Parts to the Five Senses)

E-e-e-e! Your little critters will enjoy creating their own animals as they practice correspondence and reading skills. In advance, make a copy of page 14 for each child and gather several different magazines with animal pictures. Read the labels at the bottom of the page with youngsters. Ask them to name the body part associated with each label. Have students cut out a magazine picture for each corresponding body part (eyes, paws or feet, a nose, a tongue, ears, a mouth or bill). Ask each child to match and glue each cutout to the appropriate space on the page to create a unique animal creation. Then have each child cut out the labels and glue each one in the correct space provided.

Double Vision
(Pattern Matching, Visual Discrimination)

A zoo full of bright and beautiful patterns will get youngsters thinking about different patterns found on animals. Discuss the different patterns that may be seen on zoo animals and record youngsters' answers on a chart. Then give each child the supplies listed and have him glue four of each shape onto a separate card as shown. Ask students to look at each card and then name animals that have a similar pattern. Have each child cut out each animal on his copy of page 15. Ask him to name each animal pictured and tell what pattern it should have on its body. Help him pair each card with the corresponding animal. To complete the activity, ask him to color each animal and then glue the remaining shapes to the correct animal as shown. What a match!

Materials for each child:

copy of page 15

small black construction paper triangles

small red construction paper triangles

small green construction paper squares

thin black construction paper strips

paper-punched yellow dots

4 index cards

crayons

glue

The Do-Touch Zoo!

name _____

©The Education Center, Inc. • *Investigating Science* • *Five Senses* • TEC1785

Glue here.

Look up in a tree to see my colorful feathers!

1

Booklet Pages

Use with "The Petting Zoo" on page 5.

Glue here.

Look at me! I am king of the jungle with very soft fur. Don't you agree?

2

Glue here.

In the water I swim free. My skin is rough, just like me!

3

Glue here.

Leaping out of the water is fun to me. My skin is smooth as can be!

4

The zoo has many animals to see. But not one animal feels like me!

5

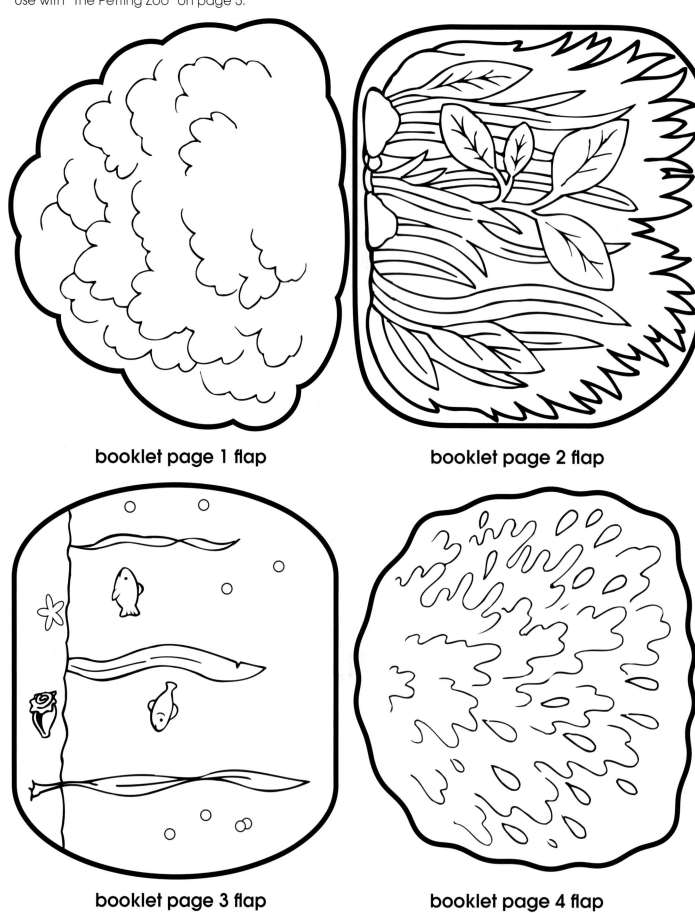

booklet page 1 flap

booklet page 2 flap

booklet page 3 flap

booklet page 4 flap

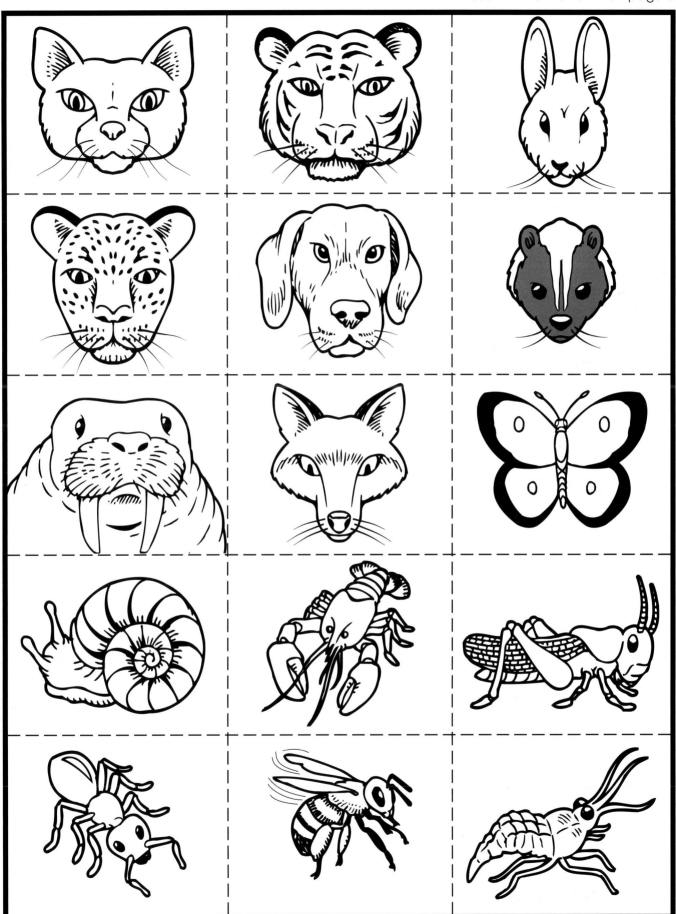

Monkey See, Monkey Do!

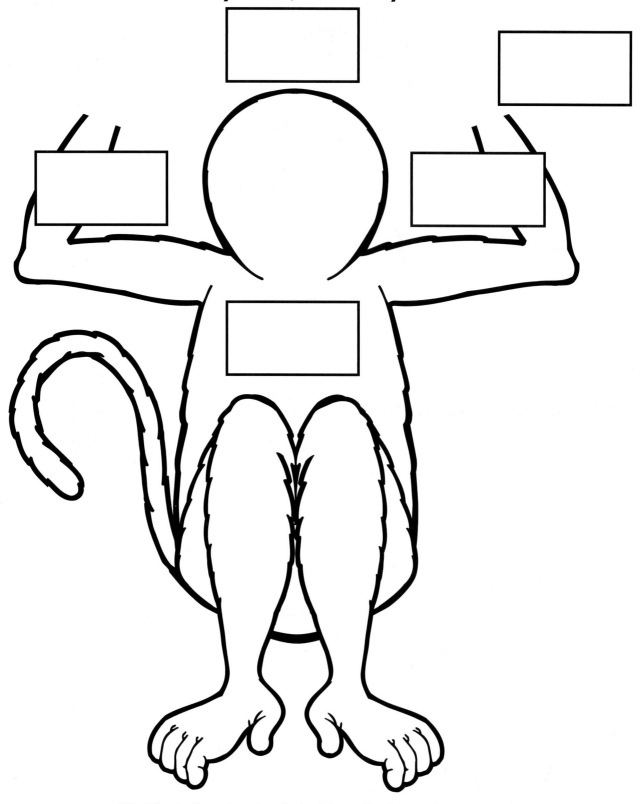

hear	see	smell	taste	touch

Note to the teacher: Use with "Monkey See, Monkey Do" on page 8.

Double Vision

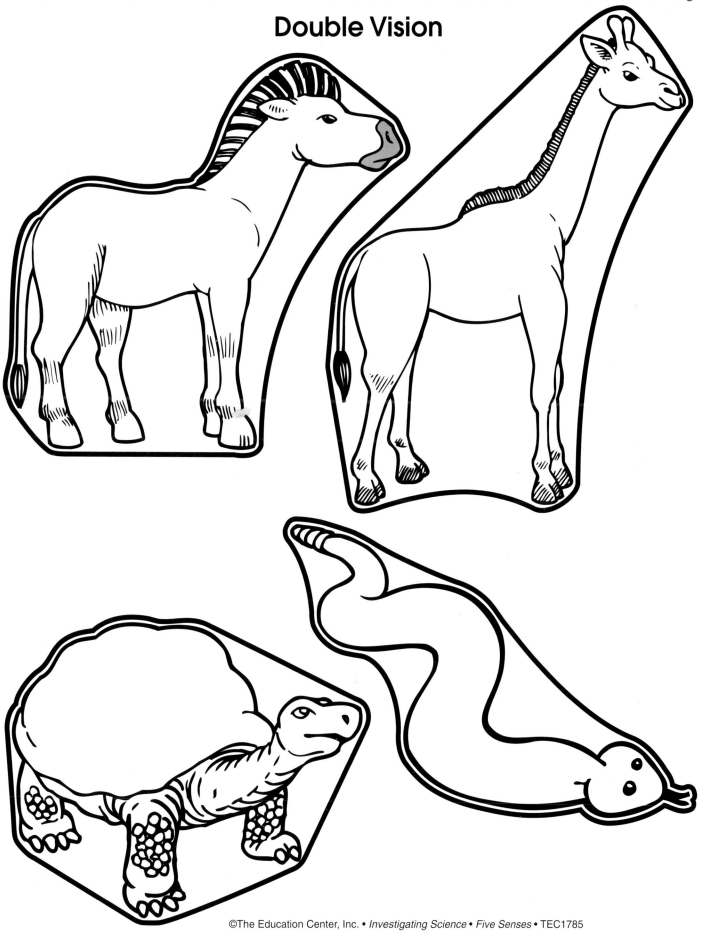

Five Senses at the Bakery

All five senses are in for a treat when youngsters visit this bakery bursting with yummy activities!

Background for the Teacher

- The five main external senses (sight, hearing, smell, taste, touch) help us understand what is happening in our environment. Each sense is controlled by a different sense organ (eyes, ears, nose, tongue, skin).
- Sight is the most important sense for learning about the world around us. We use our eyes in almost everything we do.
- Hearing makes it possible for us to communicate with others through speech. Hearing also alerts us to danger and provides pleasure such as listening to music.
- Smelling helps us recognize what is happening around us and helps us recognize food. Smell is closely related to taste because we usually smell and taste food at the same time.
- Tasting food helps determine what and how much we eat. We often smell and taste food simultaneously, so when we have a stuffy nose some foods may taste similar.
- Touching helps us determine the shape and texture of objects. We can also feel warmth, coldness, and pain through touch.

Baker Bob
(Identifying Five Senses)

Youngsters will experience the sweet smell of success in five senses identification when you introduce them to Baker Bob. In advance, gather a supply of index cards, copy page 21 to make a class supply, and enlarge one copy of page 21 to display. If desired, read to youngsters *Mr. Cookie Baker* by Monica Wellington. Direct youngsters' attention to the display and help them identify and label each of the five senses as shown. Ask your little bakers to name things found in a bakery to correspond with each of the five senses. Record each child's answer on a separate index card and have her tape it next to the corresponding label as shown. Review the list with youngsters. Then give each child a copy of page 21 and ask her to label each of the five senses, using the display as a guide.

Have each child illustrate each of the five senses on her sheet as shown. Invite youngsters to take their sheets home to introduce Baker Bob and the five senses to their families.

"Sense-sational" Books

My Five Senses by Aliki
The Pie Is Cherry by Michael Rex
Taste by Sue Hurwitz
A Tasting Party by Jane Belk-Moncure
Uncle Phil's Diner by Helena Clare Pittman

Cherries on Top
(Observing, Comparing Size, Movement)

This sweet comparison activity is as fun as a bowl of cherries! To prepare, ask a parent volunteer to create a three-inch cherry for each child by filling a red balloon with sand or rice as shown. Also collect two muffin pans, two oven mitts, two pairs of tongs, a tennis ball, a Ping-Pong ball, and a marble. Set up an unobstructed path with the muffin pans at the opposite end from the oven mitts and tongs. Begin by gathering youngsters and showing them one balloon cherry. Ask a child to choose a ball that is approximately the same size as the cherry *(tennis ball)*. Then, holding the cherry, walk several feet away from the group and show them the cherry again. Ask a different child to choose a ball that is approximately the same size as the cherry appears from that distance *(Ping-Pong ball)*. Walk even farther away and repeat the process, comparing the cherry size to a marble. Ask youngsters to hypothesize how the same cherry can appear to be different sizes; then discuss the terms *near* and *far.*

Have youngsters make further observations about *near* and *far* with this cheery cherry relay race. Divide youngsters into two teams. Model for youngsters how to put on the oven mitt and pick up one cherry with the tongs. Carefully walk to the opposite end of the path and drop the cherry into the muffin pan. Then return to the group, remove the mitt, and hand it and the tongs to the next player in line.

Sweet-Smellin' Muffins
(Identifying, Matching)

Little bakers will challenge their sense of smell with this matching center activity. To prepare, toss several cotton balls with a few drops of each extract (vanilla, peppermint, almond, maple) in separate plastic resealable bags. Glue several of each scent of cotton ball into separate cups of a paper-lined muffin pan, as shown, to make muffins. Make sure you have at least two muffins of each scent for matching. Ask a small group of youngsters to smell each muffin and then work together to sort the matching scents into pairs. Smmmells yummy!

Ring-a-ding Sprinkles
(Listening, Counting, Motor Skills)

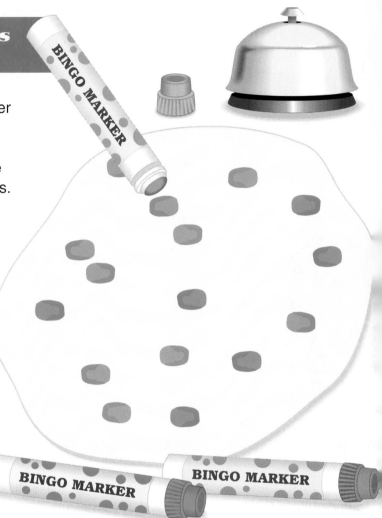

Sharpen listening skills as youngsters dab sprinkles onto a huge cookie! In advance, gather several different-colored bingo markers and a call bell; cut a large construction paper cookie for each child. Set up a divider, such as a piece of cardboard, to hide the bell and bingo markers. Have one little cookie decorator sit behind the divider with his cookie. Ask him to ring the bell each time he dabs a sprinkle onto his cookie. Have the other children listen carefully and count the number of times the bell rings. When the child is finished decorating his cookie, ask him to stand. Then ask students to tell how many sprinkles they counted. To check, have the child show his decorated cookie and count out loud the number of sprinkles on it. Ring-a-ding, ding!

Sprinkle Search
(Sorting, Patterning)

This big cookie won't crumble as youngsters use their sense of touch to practice patterning. To prepare, cut two large cookie shapes and several small circles, triangles, and squares from craft foam. Divide the small shapes into two separate paper bags and put them at a center with the cookie shapes. Also make a copy of page 22 for each child. Read the directions to students and have them complete the sheet as they wait for a turn to visit the center. Invite two students at a time to the center. Have each child choose one sprinkle pattern from her sheet to re-create. Then have her place one hand inside a bag to feel the shapes. Ask her to find, without looking at the shapes, those that correspond with her pattern. Have her duplicate the sprinkle pattern on one cookie shape. Then invite each child to repeat the process to re-create several different patterns from the sheet. Sprinkle, sprinkle, sprinkle!

May I Take Your Order?
(Communicating, Observing, Problem Solving)

This telephone tag activity is a terrific way for youngsters to practice observation and listening skills. Gather two toy telephones and cut out an assortment of magazine pictures of bakery-style foods. Choose two students to play the game: a customer and a baker. Ask the customer to choose a food picture without showing it to the baker. Have the customer pretend to call the baker and then describe the food he would like to order without calling it by name. The baker must try to guess the name of the food. Then have them swap roles and repeat the game. Place the telephones and pictures at a center so that every child may have the opportunity to play the game. Order up!

Bake a Batch
(Experimenting, Identifying, Predicting)

Junior bakers will explore all five senses as they mix up their own big cookies! Gather a class supply of paper bowls, paper towels, and the ingredients for the cookie recipe at right. Personalize a five-inch square of aluminum foil for each child. Have your little bakers wash their hands. Then invite a small group to investigate the texture, smell, and taste of each ingredient as you help them follow the recipe directions. Discuss with the group how they use their five senses as they mix up the ingredients. While the cookies are baking, help youngsters complete copies of pages 23 and 24. Mmm, smells good!

My Big Oatmeal Cookie!

(ingredients for one four-inch cookie)
¼ c. oatmeal
⅛ c. packed brown sugar
⅛ c. softened butter
⅛ c. flour
1 tbsp. raisins
pinch baking soda

1. Pour all the ingredients into your bowl and then mix them together with your hands.
2. Knead the dough until it forms a ball.
3. Place your dough ball on your foil square and flatten it. Then place the foil square on a cookie sheet.

Bake cookies at 350° for ten minutes until golden brown.

Utensil Sound Off
(Discriminating Different Sounds)

Keep them guessing with this fun sound-identification game. Gather a variety of different safe kitchen utensils and display them for all to see. Invite one child at a time to choose an item and tap it on the table to make a sound. Discuss the type of sound each utensil makes and the different sounds that come from metal, plastic, and wooden items. Then have youngsters turn away from the display so they cannot see the utensils. Have one student choose a utensil and tap it to make a sound. Ask the other students to guess which utensil made that sound. Repeat until each child has had a turn. Then have youngsters turn around and help sort the utensils by type (metal, plastic, or wood). Experiment to determine whether all the utensils in each set have similar sounds.

sticky	cake
hot	oven
crunchy	cookie
sweet	frosting

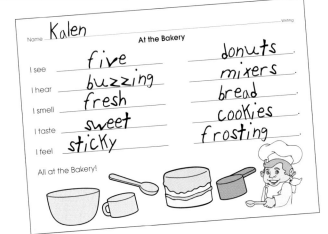

Name __Kalen__   Writing

At the Bakery

I see ___five___ ___donuts___

I hear ___buzzing___ ___mixers___

I smell ___fresh___ ___bread___

I taste ___sweet___ ___cookies___

I feel ___sticky___ ___frosting___

All at the Bakery!

Bakery Write-Off
(Recalling Information, Writing)

Call on youngsters to use their thinking skills to create a sensory poem. Make a copy of page 25 for each child. Ask students to brainstorm a list of words that describe or name things found in a bakery. Record youngsters' responses on a chart with describing words (adjectives) in one column and object words (nouns) in another column. Help each child write or dictate words to complete her copy of page 25. Then invite each child to read her descriptive writing to a partner.

Name _____

Baker Bob's Five Senses

Color.

Cut.

Match.

Glue.

taste

touch

smell

hear

see

©The Education Center, Inc. • Investigating Science • Five Senses • TEC1785

Note to the teacher: Use with "Baker Bob" on page 16.

21

Name

Sprinkle Patterns

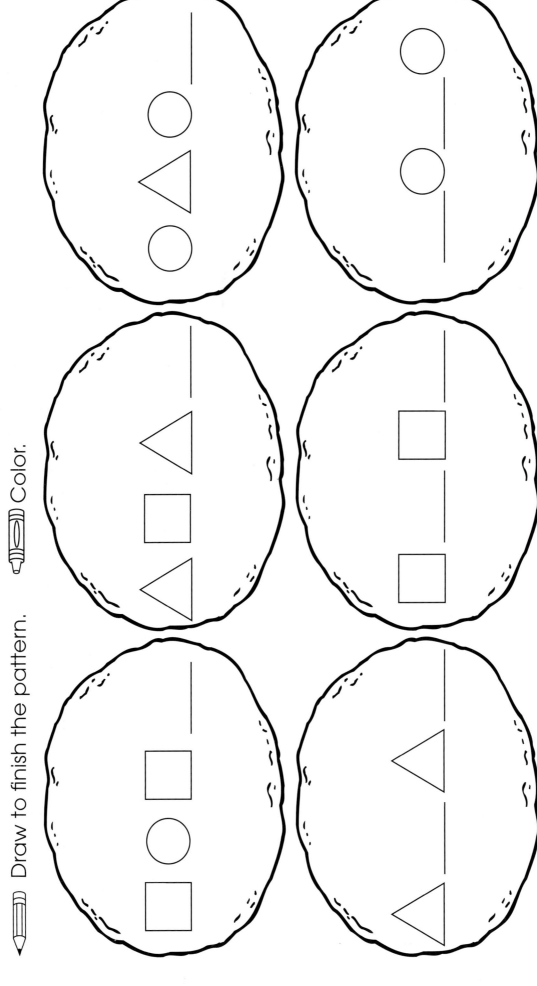

Draw to finish the pattern.

Color.

Note to the teacher: Use with "Sprinkle Search" on page 18.

Name _____

Bake a Batch

 Color.    Cut. Sequence. Glue.

1	2	3	4	5

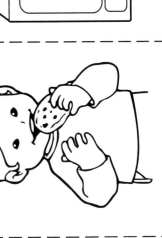

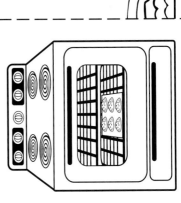

Note to the teacher: Use with "Bake a Batch" on page 19.

Mix It Up!

Count. ✏️ Write. 🖍️ Color.

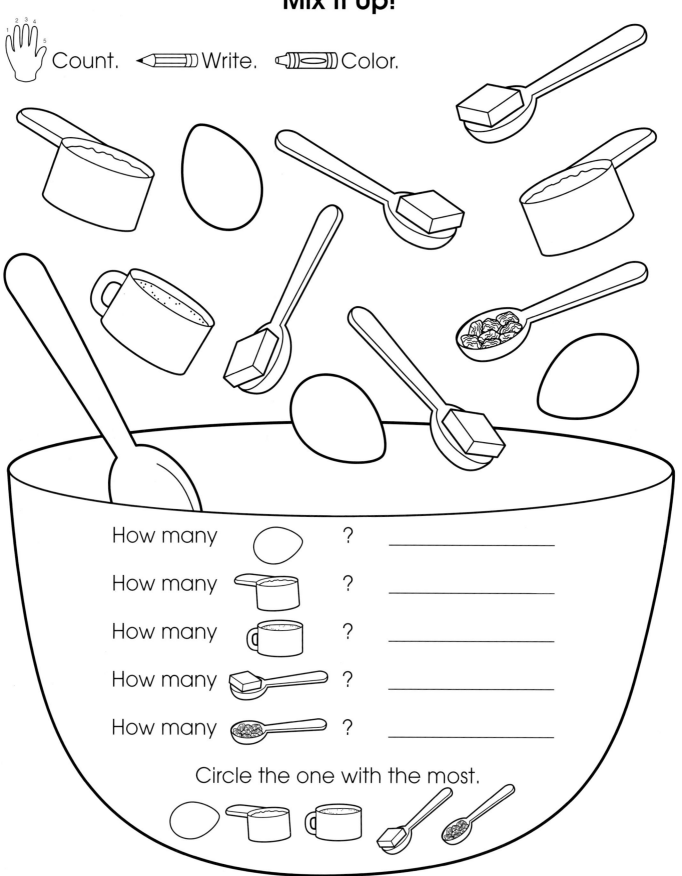

How many 🥚 ? _____

How many (measuring cup) ? _____

How many ☕ ? _____

How many (spoon) ? _____

How many (spoon with raisins) ? _____

Circle the one with the most.

Name

At the Bakery

I see _____.

I hear _____.

I smell _____.

I taste _____.

I feel _____.

All at the bakery!

Note to the teacher: Use with "Bakery Write-Off" on page 20.

Five Senses in the Garden

Tap into your little ones' sense of wonder with this garden variety of activities!

Background for the Teacher

- The five main external senses (sight, hearing, smell, taste, touch) help us understand what is happening in our environment. Each sense is controlled by a different sense organ (eyes, ears, nose, tongue, skin).
- Sight is the most important sense for learning about the world around us. We use our eyes in almost everything we do.
- Hearing makes it possible for us to communicate with others through speech. Hearing also alerts us to danger and provides pleasure such as listening to music.
- Smelling helps us recognize what is happening around us and helps us recognize food. Smell is closely related to taste because we usually smell and taste food at the same time.
- Tasting food helps determine what and how much we eat. We often smell and taste food simultaneously, so when we have a stuffy nose some foods may taste similar.
- Touching helps us determine the shape and texture of objects. We can also feel warmth, coldness, and pain through touch.

What Do You Hear?
(Sound Associations)

Your youngsters' ears are sure to perk up when they re-create sounds heard in the garden! In advance, make a class supply of page 30. Select volunteers to demonstrate the sound made by each item on the page. Then guide children to color only those items that can be heard in the garden *(hose, rain, bee, bird, cricket, shovel)*. Encourage youngsters to demonstrate other sounds associated with the garden that are not listed on the page. Then have each child complete the bonus box. Youngsters will quickly see how the garden can be a very musical place!

Fresh-Picked Titles

The Enormous Carrot by Vladimir Vagin
The Five Senses by Sally Hewitt
Garden by Robert Maass
Growing Vegetable Soup by Lois Ehlert
Planting a Rainbow by Lois Ehlert

A Garden Grab Bag
(Predicting, Using Descriptive Language)

Explore a variety of garden-related objects with this hands-on activity. In advance, line a large clay pot with a dark plastic trash bag. Place an assortment of gardening objects (such as a resealable plastic bag of soil, a small shovel, a watering can, and seeds) into a large shopping bag. Begin by asking youngsters to name objects that may be used in a garden. List responses on chart paper. Then display the clay pot. Out of the children's view, remove an item from the shopping bag and place it into the pot. Invite a volunteer to come forward, close his eyes, place his hand inside the pot, and feel the object. Encourage him to describe its texture before guessing what it is. Have the child pull the object from the pot to reveal its identity. Repeat this process with each remaining item. Save the soil until last, pouring it into the pot. Then compare the objects to the items listed on the chart. Encourage children to imagine and describe the textures of the remaining items listed on the chart.

If desired, place the clay pot and garden objects at a center to give students the opportunity for further exploration.

BEANS, LIMA 8136
Fordhook Bush #242

In a Garden

seeds	watering can
shovel	mud
hoe	bees
dirt	rabbit
flowers	bugs
vegetables	

Colorful Garden Graph

red	green	yellow
tomato	cucumber	yellow pepper
radish	green peas	squash
flower	green pepper	flower
flower		corn

Colorful Creations
(Sorting, Graphing)

Help youngsters visualize a palette of colors with this engaging activity. In advance, collect a variety of colorful flowers and vegetables, and create a class graph as shown. Invite children to sort the items into color groups. Then have students take turns drawing a different item in the appropriate section of the graph as shown. After you discuss the results, ask students what colors might be seen the most and the least in the garden. To practice graphing skills, help each child complete a copy of page 31. What a variety of colors!

Tasty Testing
(Identifying, Classifying)

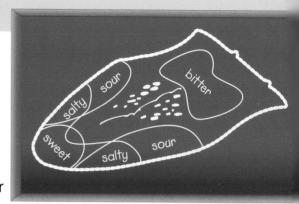

Your youngsters will have a great time munching their way through this tasty selection! Ahead of time, prepare a class supply of paper plates with a small sample of each of the following: a lemon, a lemon peel, salted lettuce, and strawberry slices. Also prepare a cup of water for each child. To begin, draw a tongue on the board labeled as shown. Explain to the children that taste buds on the tongue help us identify a taste as being sour, bitter, salty, or sweet. Next, have each youngster taste the lemon. Invite a volunteer to describe the taste and then come forward to identify the area of the tongue where the taste is the strongest. Then have her take a drink of water to help clear her mouth of any remaining lemon taste. Continue in this same manner with the remaining items.

A Scent-Filled Center
(Comparing and Identifying Scents)

Sniff, sniff, sniff. It's a matching game with just one whiff! In advance, gather several strongly scented garden items, such as onion slices, rose petals, sliced radishes, and cucumbers. Provide a magazine photo or illustration for each sample and a blindfold. Place each sample into a resealable plastic bag and then hide the bags from view in a large shopping bag. Next, label a sentence strip with one numeral for each sample, as shown. Then label a set of matching sticky notes. Place all the items at a center.

Working in pairs, one child wears the blindfold and is the tester; the other child is his helper. First, the helper selects a sample from the shopping bag and attaches the number 1 sticky note to it. She asks the tester to smell the sample and then she returns it to the shopping bag. The tester removes the blindfold, selects the photo that matches his prediction, and then places the photo on the sentence strip atop the number 1 as shown. Pairs continue in this same manner until all items have been tested. The helper then displays the samples from the shopping bag. Have the pair compare the tester's answers with the correct answers. Then remove the sticky notes and have the pair switch roles. Hey, I know that smell!

"Sense-sational" Soup
(Comparing and Contrasting the Five Senses)

Create a feast for the senses with this mouthwatering activity. In advance, gather the ingredients listed below for making vegetable soup. Also, make a class supply of the recipe on page 32. Share the story *Growing Vegetable Soup* by Lois Ehlert with youngsters. Explain to the class that they will be making vegetable soup to enjoy. Then distribute a copy of the recipe to each child.

To prepare the soup, enlist the help of the children to complete Step 1 by washing the vegetables. Encourage them to discuss various sensory experiences as they help complete this step *(such as the water feels cold and it makes a splashing sound)*. Next, ask each child to circle the symbols on her page that represent the senses used in Step 1. Proceed through the remaining steps, continuing the process of identifying and circling the senses used. Mmm, Mmm, good!

Ingredients:

variety of fresh vegetables
access to running water
cutting board
2 large cans chicken broth

2 qt. pot
access to a stove
ladle
bowls
spoons

Steps:
1. Wash vegetables.
2. Cut vegetables.
3. Fill pot ⅔ full of water and chicken broth.
4. Add vegetables.
5. Cook until vegetables soften.
6. Eat!

In the Garden
(sung to the tune of "Frère Jacques")

In the garden, in the garden,
I can smell, I can smell
Sweet-scented flowers, sweet-scented flowers.
Sniff, sniff, sniff.
Sniff, sniff, sniff.
In the garden, in the garden,
I can see, I can see
Bright colors blooming, bright colors blooming.
Blink, blink, blink.
Blink, blink, blink.
In the garden, in the garden,
I can hear, I can hear
Bees that are buzzing, bees that are buzzing.
Buzz, buzz, buzz.
Buzz, buzz, buzz.
In the garden, in the garden,
I can feel, I can feel
Thorns on the roses, thorns on the roses.
Ouch, ouch, ouch.
Ouch, ouch, ouch.
In the garden, in the garden,
I can taste, I can taste
Veggies that are yummy, veggies that are yummy.
Crunch, crunch, crunch.
Crunch, crunch, crunch.

Garden Review
(Language, Music)

This little ditty will have youngsters tapping out the beats as they review sense-filled garden treats! Give each child the materials listed to create a garden visor. Help each child dip a finger in paint and then press three fingerprints in the space above the fence. After the paint dries, ask him to decorate the fingerprints to resemble flowers as shown. Have him color and cut out his visor. Help him hole-punch the two black dots and then thread the yarn through the holes. Tie the visor to fit the child's head. Encourage each child to wear his visor as the class sings the song at left.

Materials for each child:

copy of page 33
paint in a shallow pan
crayons

scissors
30" length of yarn
access to a hole puncher

Name _____

Garden Sounds

Bonus Box: On the back of this sheet, finish the sentence "In the garden I can hear…" Draw a picture to match the sentence.

©The Education Center, Inc. • *Investigating Science • Five Senses • TEC1785*

Note to the teacher: Use with "What Do You Hear?" on page 26.

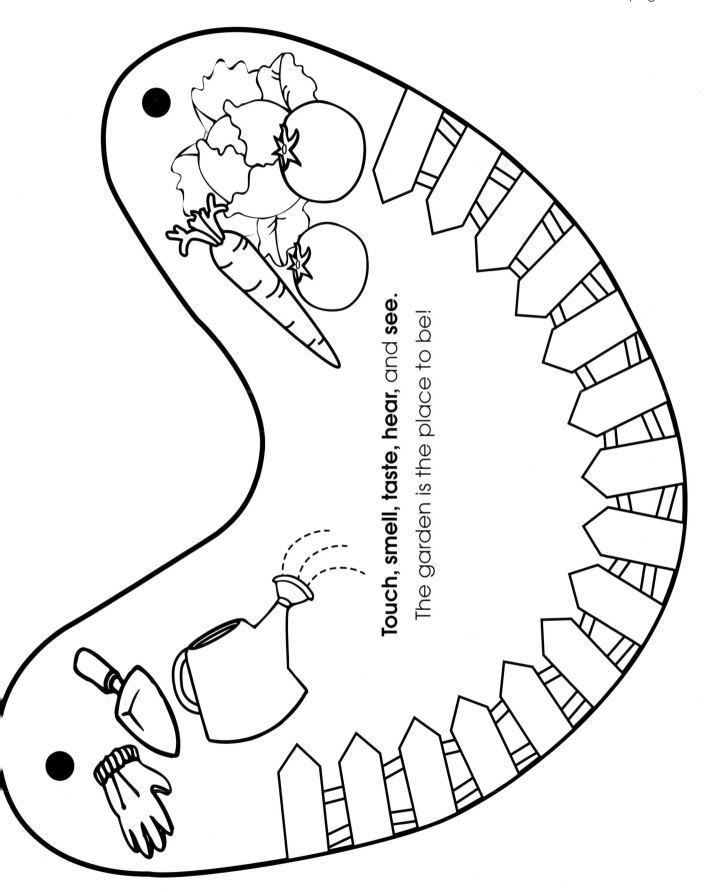

Touch, smell, **taste, hear,** and **see.**

The garden is the place to be!

Five Senses in the Woods

Invite your youngsters on a journey to discover the wonders of the woods with this collection of sensory-inspired activities!

Background for the Teacher

- The five main external senses (sight, hearing, smell, taste, touch) help us understand what is happening in our environment. Each sense is controlled by a different sense organ (eyes, ears, nose, tongue, skin).
- Sight is the most important sense for learning about the world around us. We use our eyes in almost everything we do.
- Hearing makes it possible for us to communicate with others through speech. Hearing also alerts us to danger and provides pleasure such as listening to music.
- Smelling helps us recognize what is happening around us and helps us recognize food. Smell is closely related to taste because we usually smell and taste food at the same time.
- Tasting food helps determine what and how much we eat. We often smell and taste food simultaneously, so when we have a stuffy nose some foods may taste similar.
- Touching helps us determine the shape and texture of objects. We can also feel warmth, coldness, and pain through touch.

"Beary" Good Senses
(Following Directions, Identifying Senses)

Reinforce listening skills and introduce the five senses with this "beary" fun art activity. Give each child a copy of "'Beary' Good Senses" on page 39 and then guide him through the following directions and questions.

Directions:

1. Color and cut out the ears, eyes, nose, and mouth and tongue.
2. Glue the eyes onto the face. Which sense uses the eyes? *(sight)*
3. Glue the nose in the middle of the face. Which sense uses the nose? *(smell)*
4. Glue the ears on the head. Which sense uses the ears? *(hearing)*
5. Glue the mouth and tongue under the nose. Which sense uses the tongue? *(taste)*
6. Which sense is missing? *(touch)*
7. In the first box draw something found in the woods that feels soft.
8. In the second box draw something found in the woods that feels hard.

Tales of the Woods

Counting on the Woods by George Ella Lyon
Forest Friends' Five Senses by Cristina Garelli
Hide and Seek by Toni Eugene
One Small Square: Woods by Donald M. Silver
Where Once There Was a Wood by Denise Fleming

What's Inside?
(Identifying Sounds, Matching)

Your youngsters will perk up their ears and get shakin' with this fun listening exercise. To prepare, collect four small crayon boxes and four different items found in the woods (such as dirt, stones, grass, acorns, seeds, or small sticks). Avoid choosing items that may sound similar when shaken. Place a different item in each box and then cover it with Con-Tact paper. Next, create a simple drawing of each item on an index card as shown. For self-checking, place a sticker on the back of each card and a matching sticker on the corresponding box. Show youngsters the cards and discuss where these types of things would be found in the woods. Place the boxes and cards at a center. Invite each child to listen to the different sounds as she shakes each box. Ask her to try to identify each sound by matching each box with a card. To self-check, have the student match corresponding stickers. Shake, listen, and match!

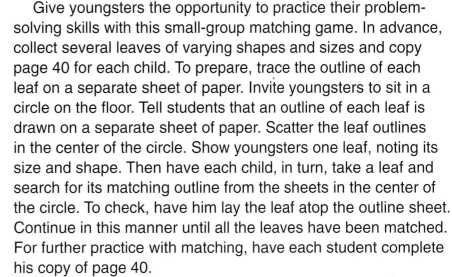

Leaf Mates
(Visual Discrimination, Matching)

Give youngsters the opportunity to practice their problem-solving skills with this small-group matching game. In advance, collect several leaves of varying shapes and sizes and copy page 40 for each child. To prepare, trace the outline of each leaf on a separate sheet of paper. Invite youngsters to sit in a circle on the floor. Tell students that an outline of each leaf is drawn on a separate sheet of paper. Scatter the leaf outlines in the center of the circle. Show youngsters one leaf, noting its size and shape. Then have each child, in turn, take a leaf and search for its matching outline from the sheets in the center of the circle. To check, have him lay the leaf atop the outline sheet. Continue in this manner until all the leaves have been matched. For further practice with matching, have each student complete his copy of page 40.

Warm Woodsy Treat
(Following Directions, Similarities and Differences)

Enlist the help of your little woodsmen to prepare this sensory treat. In advance, ask a parent to send in enough refrigerated sugar cookie dough for each student to have a piece of dough the size of a Ping-Pong ball. (One 18-ounce package makes approximately 21 cookies.) Also copy page 41 and personalize a square of aluminum foil for each child. Then prepare a plate sprinkled with ⅓ cup of cinnamon sugar for each small group of students. Ask students to name different things found in the woods, such as snakes, trees, leaves, and acorns. Have youngsters wash their hands. Then spray the hands of a small group of students with nonstick cooking spray. Give each student in the group a ball of dough. Then ask the students to form their dough balls into their favorite woodsy objects and then place them on top of their foil squares. Encourage youngsters to feel the texture of the dough and smell the sweet aroma of the cinnamon sugar. Next, have them take turns placing their creations into the cinnamon sugar. Encourage them to notice how the dough changes color and to listen to the crunching sound made on the plate. Bake the cookies according to the package instructions. As the cookies bake, help students complete a copy of page 41. Then give youngsters their warm cookies and ask them to use their five senses to describe the similarities and differences between the cookie dough and the baked cookie. Record youngsters' observations on a chart as shown. Mmmm good!

Dough	Cookie
sticky	soft
sweet	sweet
cold	warm
white	brown

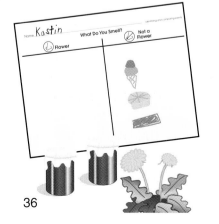

The Nose Knows
(Identifying and Comparing Scents)

Can youngsters distinguish one smell from another? Challenge them with this experiment to discover what the nose really knows! In advance, copy page 42 for each child and collect several film canisters, cheesecloth, and rubber bands. Then gather two types of fragrant items: flower scented and some that do not smell like flowers. (See the list below for suggestions.) To prepare, place a sample of each item in a separate canister and then cover each one with cheesecloth secured with a rubber band as shown. For self-checking, attach a sticker to the bottom of each canister containing a flower-scented sample. Place the canisters, copies of page 42, and crayons at a center. Direct each child to sniff a canister, decide whether it smells like a flower, and then place the canister on the corresponding side of the chart. To self-check, have her look for a sticker under each flower-scented canister. Then have her draw a picture of what each sample that did not smell like flowers reminds her of as shown.

Smells Like Flowers	Does Not Smell Like Flowers
herbal tea bag	baby powder
perfume	powdered drink mix
lotion	vanilla extract
herbal shampoo	cinnamon
potpourri	dryer sheet
soap	hot chocolate mix

36

Through an Animal's Eyes
(Demonstration, Simulation)

Give your students the opportunity to see the world through the eyes of a few woods-dwelling animals with this demonstration. In advance, gather a pair of binoculars, a small hand mirror, and two foam cups with the bottoms cut out. Cover the top of each cup with blue acetate and secure with a rubber band. Label each item as shown and then place the items on a table. Explain to students that the items are labeled with the names of three animals that can be found in the woods. Tell them that each animal uses its eyes to see things in a different way. The owl is able to swivel its head around to look backward, allowing it to see in all directions. Have a student hold the hand mirror and turn with his back to the class. Help him simulate an owl's vision by having him look into the mirror and focus on the class behind him. Ask youngsters how the owl's vision helps it survive. *(It can scan a large area for prey.)* Next, tell students the eagle can see faraway objects clearly. Then help a student simulate an eagle's vision by having him look into the binoculars and focus on something that is distant. Ask youngsters how the eagle's vision helps it survive. *(It can see prey that is far away.)* Tell students that a bee cannot focus its eyes and it can't see red. But it can see blue and patterns of flowers. Have a student look through the cups to pretend to be a bee!

Caw! Caw!

Hoo! Hoo!

Crunch!

Ribbit!

Name That Sound
(Identifying Sounds, Communicating Through Movement)

Here's a fun way for students to put their sense of hearing to work as they try to identify common sounds heard in the woods. In advance, obtain a recording of common nature sounds, such as birds, crickets, owls, bees, wind, crunching leaves, and flowing streams. Review the recording ahead of time to identify each sound. Play the recording for the children, stopping after each sound. Encourage students to identify what they heard. Then invite students to imitate the source of each sound through movement. Continue in the same manner until all sounds have been identified. That sure sounds like fun!

Sensory Stamping
(Fine-Motor Skills, Art)

Youngsters will surely be in touch with their senses when they use woodsy objects to stamp beautiful creations. In advance, gather various nature items (such as pinecones, leaves, tufts of grass, and flowers), paint, bowls, and paper. Next, pour a different color of paint into a shallow bowl for each collected item. Invite a small group of children to the center. Help each child create a nature painting by dipping each item into the paint and then stamping it onto his paper. Encourage him to use each different item, overlapping shapes if necessary. When the pictures are dry, display them on a bulletin board titled "Naturally Beautiful."

Five Senses Stroll
(Exploring the Senses)

Challenge youngsters to use their senses as they investigate the great outdoors with a nature walk. In advance, copy page 43 for each child and gather several magnifying glasses. Then encourage youngsters to brainstorm a list of sights, sounds, smells, textures, and tastes that might be found in the woods. Record their answers on a chart as shown. Invite youngsters to take a sensory stroll outdoors. (Before beginning the walk, discuss important safety rules, reminding them that using their sense of taste in the woods is unsafe.) If possible, lead your youngsters through a wooded area, encouraging them to comment on what they see, hear, and smell. During the walk, collect several items that are safe for students to investigate. Later, give each child an opportunity to use a magnifying glass to explore the collected items and describe how they look, smell, and feel. Youngsters will quickly realize how important their senses are in learning more about the world around them. To help youngsters review the five senses, have them complete a copy of page 43.

See	Hear	Smell	Feel	Taste
squirrels	birds singing	flowers	bark	berries
trees	water flowing	pine needles	sticks	nuts
leaves	bees buzzing		grass	

"Beary" Good Senses

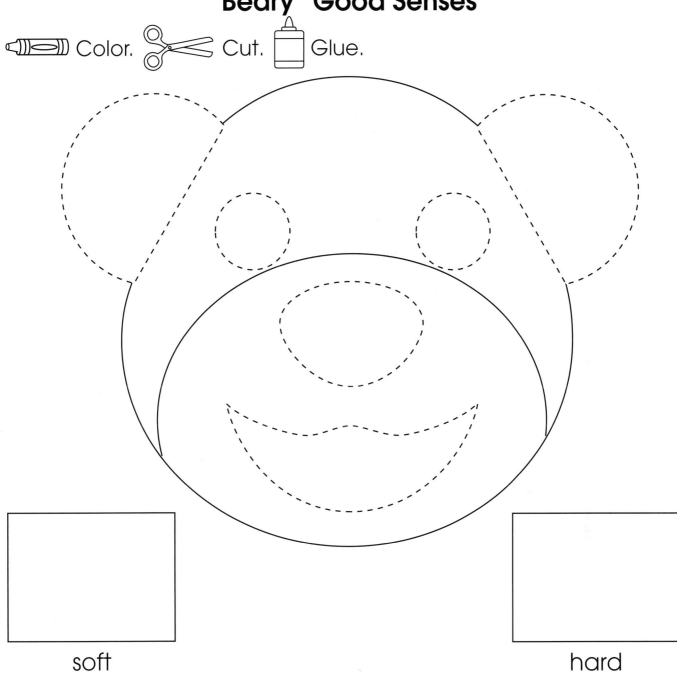

🖍 Color. ✂ Cut. 🧴 Glue.

soft   hard

©The Education Center, Inc. • *Investigating Science* • *Five Senses* • TEC1785

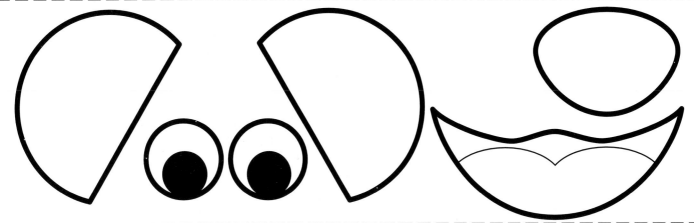

In the Woods

🖍️ Color. ✂️ Cut. 🧴 Glue.

Note to the teacher: Use with "Leaf Mates" on page 35.

Name _____

Woodsy Wonders

Look at each picture. Circle the senses being used. Color.

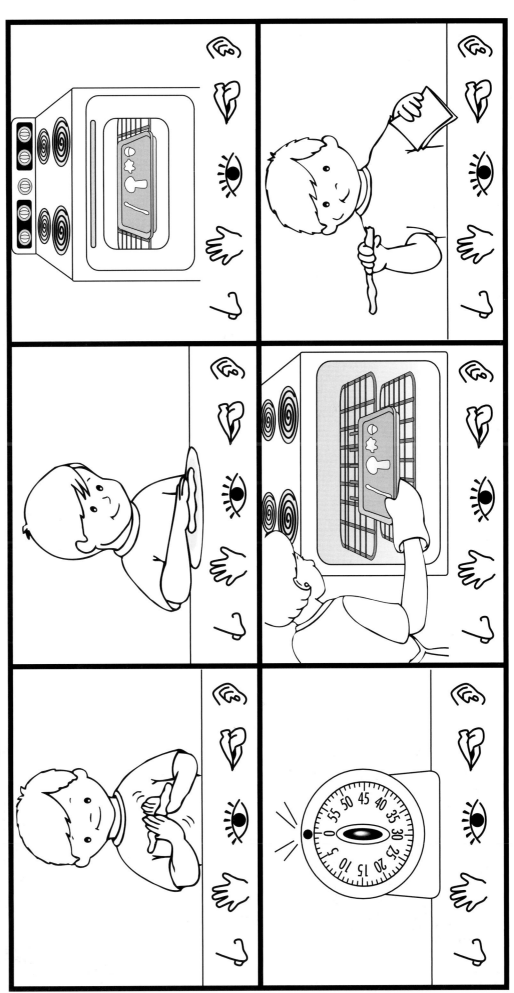

©The Education Center, Inc. • Investigating Science • Five Senses • TEC1785

Note to the teacher: Use with "Warm Woodsy Treat" on page 36.

Name _____

What Do You Smell?

Flower

Not a Flower

Note to the teacher: Use with "The Nose Knows" on page 36.

Senses All Around

Look at each picture. Decide which sense is being used.

 Color each picture according to the color code.

👁—red   👃—blue   ✋—green   👂—yellow   👅—orange

Bonus Box: On the back of this sheet, draw your favorite things to smell, taste, touch, hear, and see.

Five Senses at Home

Home, sweet home! Show youngsters that they do not have to go far to explore their five senses.

Background for the Teacher

- The five main external senses (sight, hearing, smell, taste, touch) help us understand what is happening in our environment. Each sense is controlled by a different sense organ (eyes, ears, nose, tongue, skin).
- Sight is the most important sense for learning about the world around us. We use our eyes in almost everything we do.
- Hearing makes it possible for us to communicate with others through speech. Hearing also alerts us to danger and provides pleasure such as listening to music.
- Smelling helps us recognize what is happening around us and helps us recognize food. Smell is closely related to taste because we usually smell and taste food at the same time.
- Tasting food helps determine what and how much we eat. We often smell and taste food simultaneously, so when we have a stuffy nose some foods may taste similar.
- Touching helps us determine the shape and texture of objects. We can also feel warmth, coldness, and pain through touch.

Right at Home With Books

The Five Senses by Carey Molter
Is It Rough? Is It Smooth? Is It Shiny? by Tana Hoban
Mr. Pine's Purple House by Leonard Kessler
My Home by Tammy K. Schlepp
Understanding Your Senses by Rebecca Treays

There's No Place Like Home!
(Categorizing, Fine Motor)

Youngsters will feel right at home during this investigation of sight. In advance, create a chart by drawing two large overlapping shapes (house and triangle) on bulletin board paper and then labeling them as shown. Ask youngsters to cut out magazine pictures of things they might see inside and outside their homes. Ask youngsters to bring their pictures with them to group time. Have one child at a time show his pictures. Ask the group to help him decide where each pictured item is found (inside, outside, or both). Then help him attach each picture to the corresponding area on the chart. Repeat the activity until each child has had a turn. To review the chart, ask a child to count how many pictures are in each category. Later send each child home with a copy of "Senses Homework" (page 47). Ask him to draw objects he observes at home to complete the page. Ask each child to return his homework and review the five senses as he shares it with classmates.

Mystery Texture Match
(Classifying, Home Activity)

Put youngsters in touch with their sense of touch! In advance, make a class supply of the parent note shown; then, for each child, place a copy inside a resealable plastic bag to send home. When all the items have been collected, have youngsters help sort them into tactile categories (rough, smooth, bumpy, soft, hard) and label each set as shown. Place one sample of each texture inside a mystery bag. Then blindfold one child and place one textured item in her hand. Ask her to reach into the mystery bag with the opposite hand to search for a matching texture. Continue until each child has had a chance to solve a mystery. Save the samples to use with "Touchable Quilt" below.

rough   smooth   bumpy   soft

hard

Dear Parent,
Please help your child find one small item for each of the following textures and place them in this bag. The items will be used for a classification activity and a craft at school.

• rough • smooth • hard • soft
• bumpy

Touchable Quilt
(Following Directions, Craft)

Youngsters create a touchable class quilt with this texture craft. To prepare, cut a class supply of different-colored construction paper house shapes as shown. Place the samples collected from "Mystery Texture Match" (above) on a table. If necessary, add texture samples so that there is a good variety (sandpaper, cotton, feathers, buttons, paper clips). Provide each child with a paper cutout and glue. Then ask a small group at a time to choose five samples to match each category (rough, smooth, bumpy, soft, hard). Have each child glue his samples onto his cutout. Allow the cutouts to dry. Arrange and glue each cutout onto a large sheet of bulletin board paper. Display the quilt with the title shown.

Our Class Touchable Texture Quilt

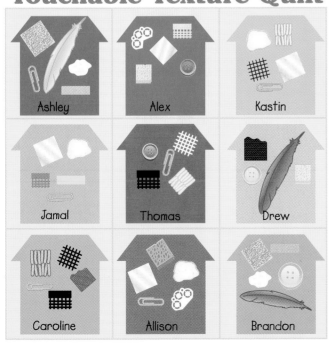

Ashley   Alex   Kastin

Jamal   Thomas   Drew

Caroline   Allison   Brandon

My Jazzy Jacket
(Listening, Art)

Listening is the key to this sense-related activity. In advance, copy page 48 for each child. Also gather a variety of flat, textured materials (sandpaper, fabric, plastic canvas) and crayon pieces with the paper covers removed. Model for youngsters how to color a texture rubbing. Then play some music that has a variety of tempos. Ask youngsters to listen to the music, pointing out how some music sounds slow paced and some music sounds fast paced. Replay the music and ask each child to create different texture rubbings on her jacket copy according to the speed of the tune. Encourage her to color quickly during the fast-paced music and then to color slowly during the slow-paced music. Ask youngsters to name the senses they used during the activity *(hearing, touch, sight)*. Then have each child cut out and take home her colorful jacket.

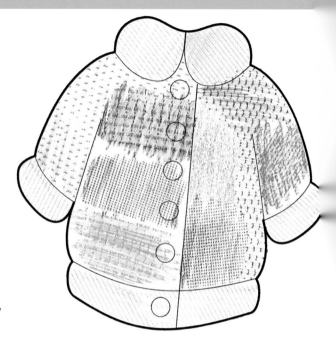

Crunch, Crunch, Munch!
(Song, Reviewing the Five Senses)

Raid the refrigerator to find crunchy foods for this delicious song as youngsters review their five senses! If desired, give youngsters samples (apple slices, carrots, crackers, etc.) to smell and taste. Help students substitute foods and descriptive words as you repeat the song.

(sung to the tune of "Twinkle, Twinkle, Little Star")

Look at the [apple] I've found.	*(Point to eyes.)*
It is [red] and it feels [smooth].	*(Pretend to hold it.)*
The [sweet] smell is tempting me.	*(Pretend to smell it.)*
What a treat it will soon be!	
Next, I'll take a bite and hear	*(Pretend to take a bite.)*
A crunch, crunch sound in my ear.	*(Hold hand to ear.)*
It tastes good; here's how I know:	
My sense of taste has told me so.	*(Point to mouth.)*
All my senses I used just now.	
Listen and I'll tell you how.	*(Chant the senses.)*
Sight!	*(Point to eyes.)*
Touch!	*(Hold up hands.)*
Smell!	*(Point to nose.)*
Hearing!	*(Point to ears.)*
Taste!	*(Point to mouth.)*

Senses Homework

✏️ Draw things at home.

At home I...

see 👁️ 👁️	touch ✋	taste 👄
smell 👃	hear 👂 👂	

©The Education Center, Inc. • *Investigating Science • Five Senses* • TEC1785

Note to the teacher: Use with "There's No Place Like Home!" on page 44.

Pattern
Use with "My Jazzy Jacket" on page 46.